Galápagos

Poems by John Delaney
Photographs by Andrew Delaney

Finishing Line Press
Georgetown, Kentucky

Galápagos

Copyright © 2023 by John Delaney
ISBN 979-8-88838-361-2 First Edition
All rights reserved under International and Pan-American Copyright Conventions.
No part of this book may be reproduced in any manner whatsoever without written permission from the publisher, except in the case of brief quotations embodied in critical articles and reviews.

ACKNOWLEDGMENTS

Grateful appreciation is due the editors of the following magazines where some of the poems and photographs first appeared:

Grey Sparrow Journal: "Galápagos Land Iguana" and bottom photo
Sisyphus: "Waved Albatross" and photos

Publisher: Leah Huete de Maines
Editor: Christen Kincaid
Cover art and photographs of Galápagos wildlife and settings: Andrew Delaney
Author/photographer photo: Omar Medina
Cover design: John Delaney

Order online: www.finishinglinepress.com
also available on amazon.com

Author inquiries and mail orders:
Finishing Line Press
PO Box 1626
Georgetown, Kentucky 40324
USA

Table of Contents

Volcano Cookies 1

Giant Tortoise 3

Galápagos Green Sea Turtle 5

Sally Lightfoot Crab 7

Galápagos Land Iguana 9

Flightless Cormorant 11

Darwin's Finches 13

Galápagos Sea Lion 15

Galápagos Penguin 17

Frigate Bird 19

Marine Iguana 21

Waved Albatross 23

Blue-Footed Booby 25

Dedicated to the Will to Survive

Considering the small size of the islands, we feel the more astonished at the number of their aboriginal beings, and at their confined range. Seeing every height crowned with its crater, and the boundaries of most of the lava-streams still distinct, we are led to believe that within a period geologically recent the unbroken ocean was here spread out. Hence, both in space and time, we seem to be brought somewhat near to that great fact—that mystery of mysteries—the first appearance of new beings on this earth.

—Charles Darwin, *The Voyage of the Beagle* (1839):
Chapter XVII, "Galápagos Archipelago"

Volcano Cookies

Magma oozes up
from the ocean's hot spot
into lava batter here,
plopped on the crust's production line,
as it drifts east-southeast
towards the coast
at five centimeters per year.

The Humboldt Current
adds nutrients
from the south, the Cromwell
from the west,
creating environments
delicate and diverse
within a finch's distance.

Islands sloughed off the belt
like volcano cookies,
each with its own patina:
Española, San Cristobal,
Floreana, Santa Cruz,
Santiago, Isabela,
Fernandina . . .

In this Equatorial kitchen
baking still flourishes;
for several million years
the recipe has repeated the process.
Word of mouth encourages
tourists' hunger:
they come to consume these Galápagos.

This map of the Galápagos Islands was drawn and engraved by Emanuel Bowen and appeared in John Harris's Navigantium Atque Itinerantium Bibliotheca *(London, 1744). From the author's personal collection.*

Giant Tortoise

The huge humps move
with the deliberation
of old men on walkers.

Occasionally, they convene
in a semi-circle
like a support group,

and reminisce
about Charlie D—how he
tried to coax them out of their shells—
whom they still miss.

The big questions
they grapple in the grass
mouthful by mouthful.

It will take a long time
to get where they're going,
so no one's in a hurry.

These giant tortoises can go for more than six months without food or water. In the wild they can live for well over one hundred years.

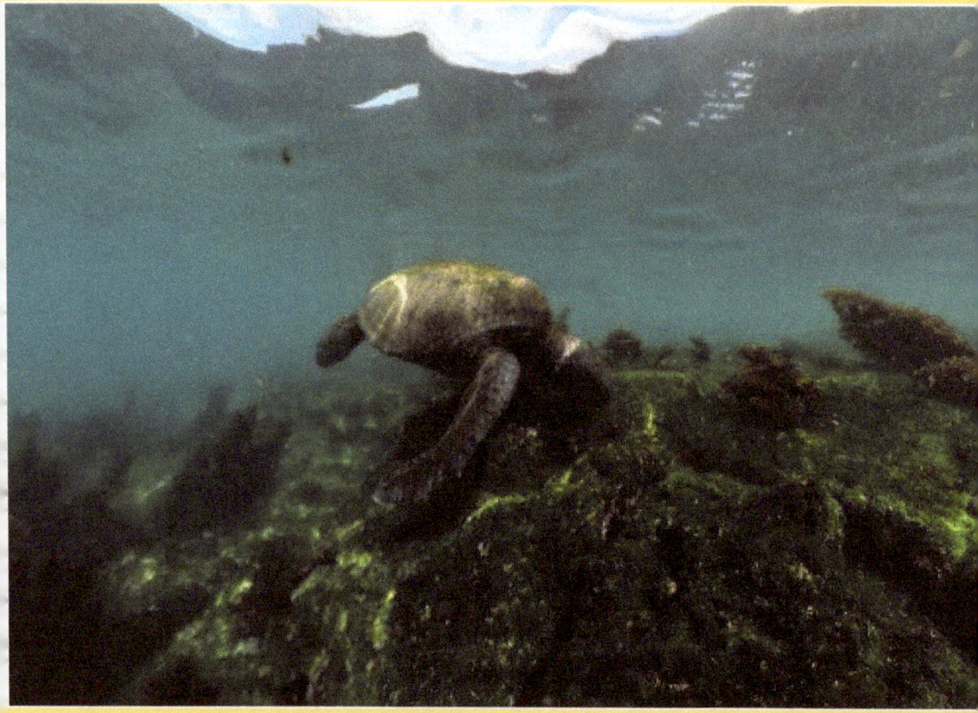
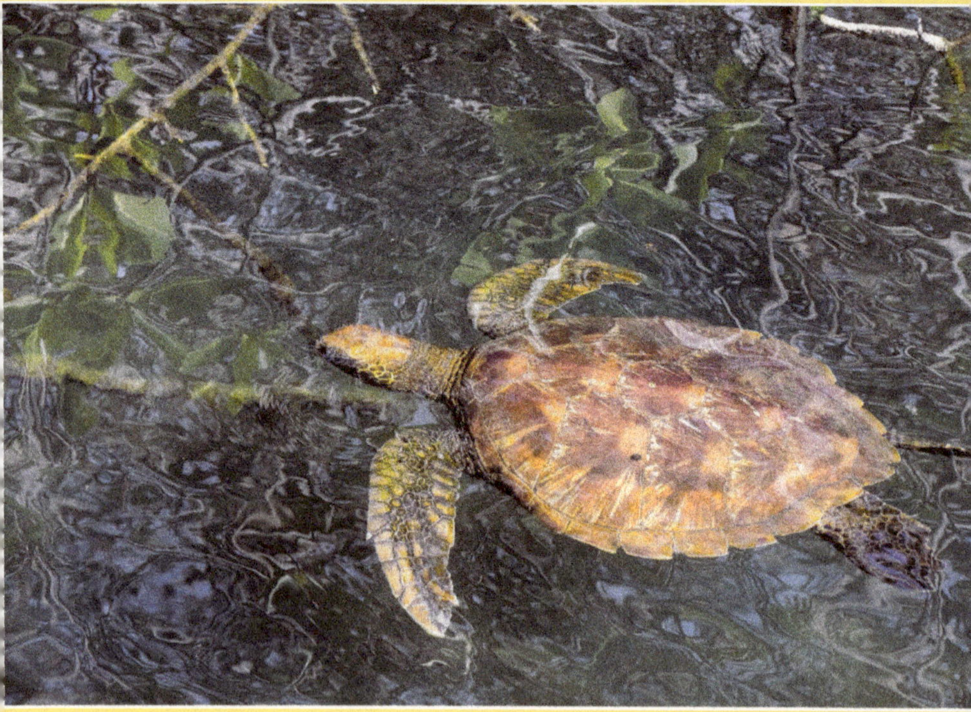

Galápagos Green Sea Turtle

I swim between worlds like a messenger.
What does each say to the other?
The sun is bright and the air is warm.
That you can breathe freely here.

But hold your breath and behold the depths
of weightlessness and wonder,
where a banquet table bares its spread.
Float as in a slow-motion dream.

I come up for air, descend to eat,
and pretend there's nothing to it
but a routine that's been perfected
from a past too distant to remember.

Back and forth I am pulled
by the present, by the future,
by the message of the medium—
that my life's a precious premium.

The Galapagos Green Sea Turtle is the only species of sea turtle to nest there. Its name comes from the color of the turtle's fat.

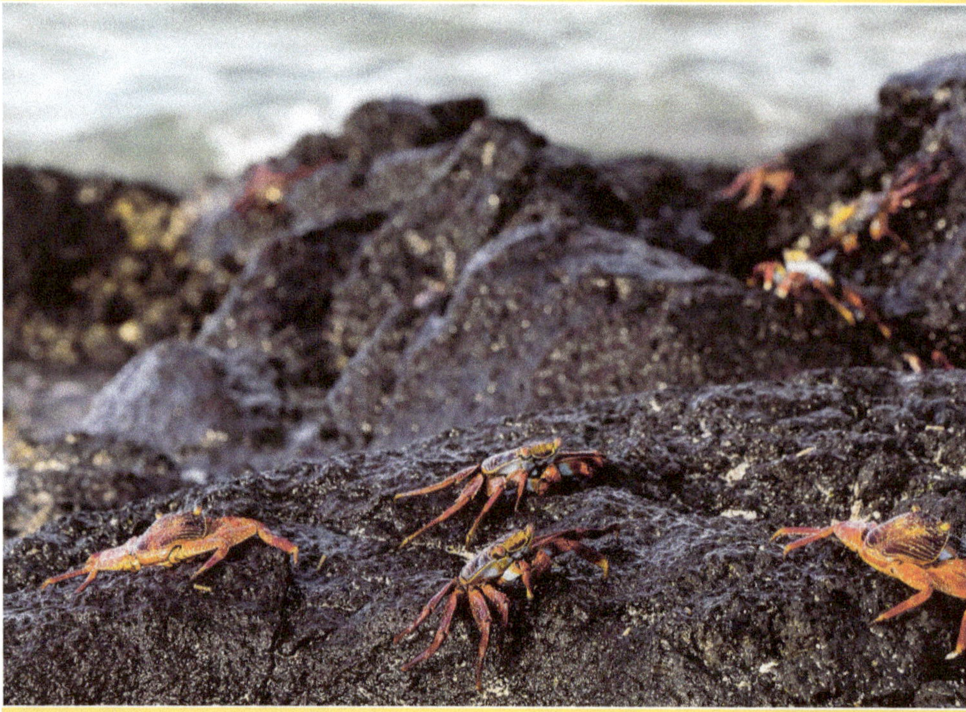

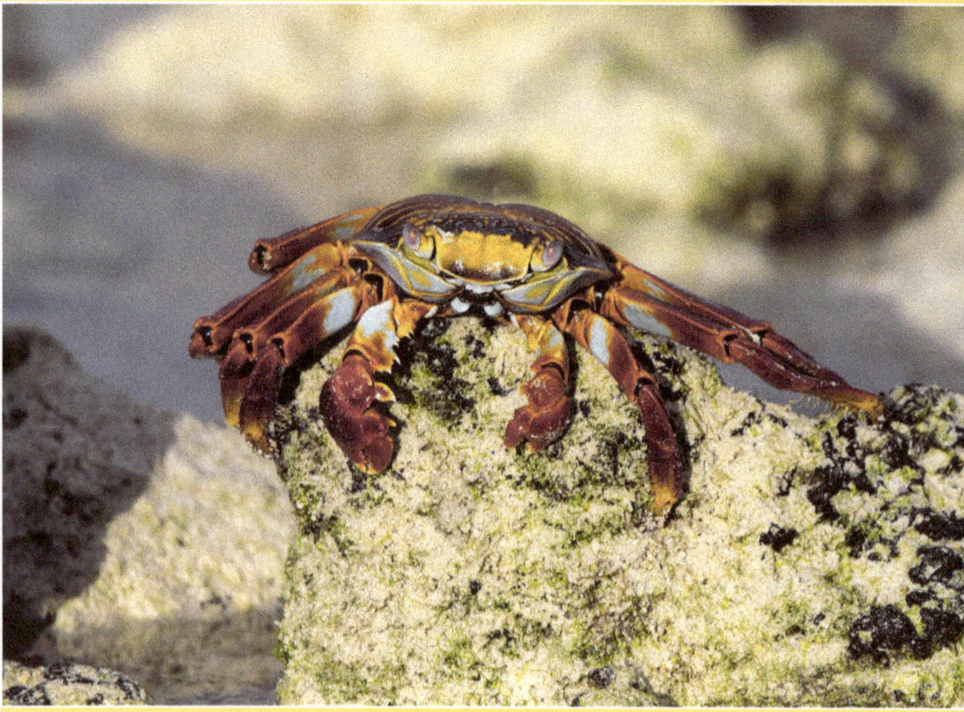

Sally Lightfoot Crab

Scattering, clattering over the rocks,
seeking a niche or a nook
beyond the turbulence of the shore
and the ocean's spray.

Scampering, clambering for algae
around lava pools and crevasses
on five pairs of skittish legs
in bright orange prison fatigues.

Scavenging, clawing a course
among coastal detritus
for a consumptuous crumb
to sate its monstrous maw.

Scratching, clutching each day;
hopping, skipping, jumping
its getaway. No pas de deux,
this hardship hobo dances solo.

Apparently named after a Caribbean dancer's agility and lightfoot way of dancing.

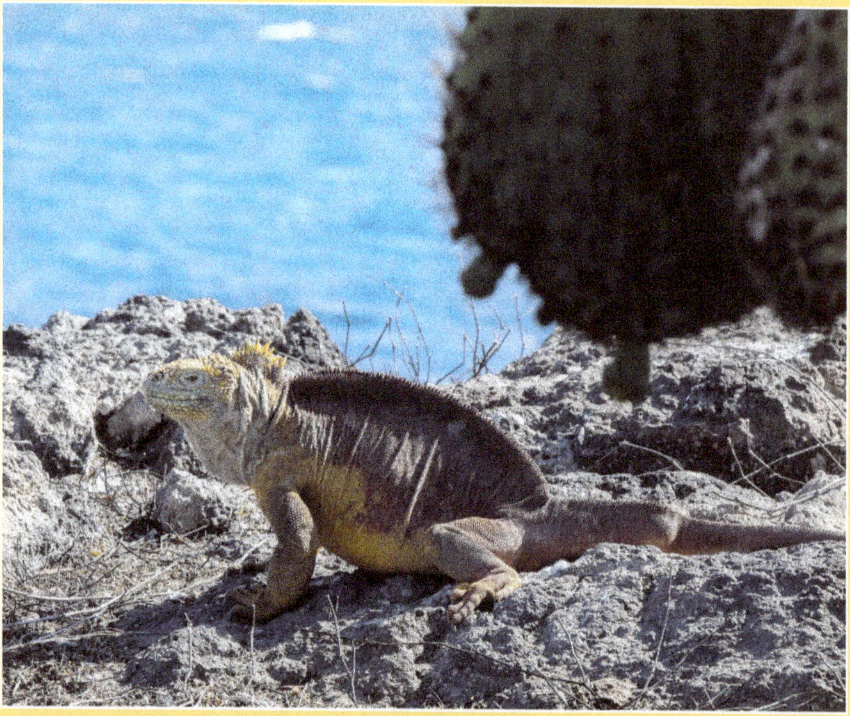

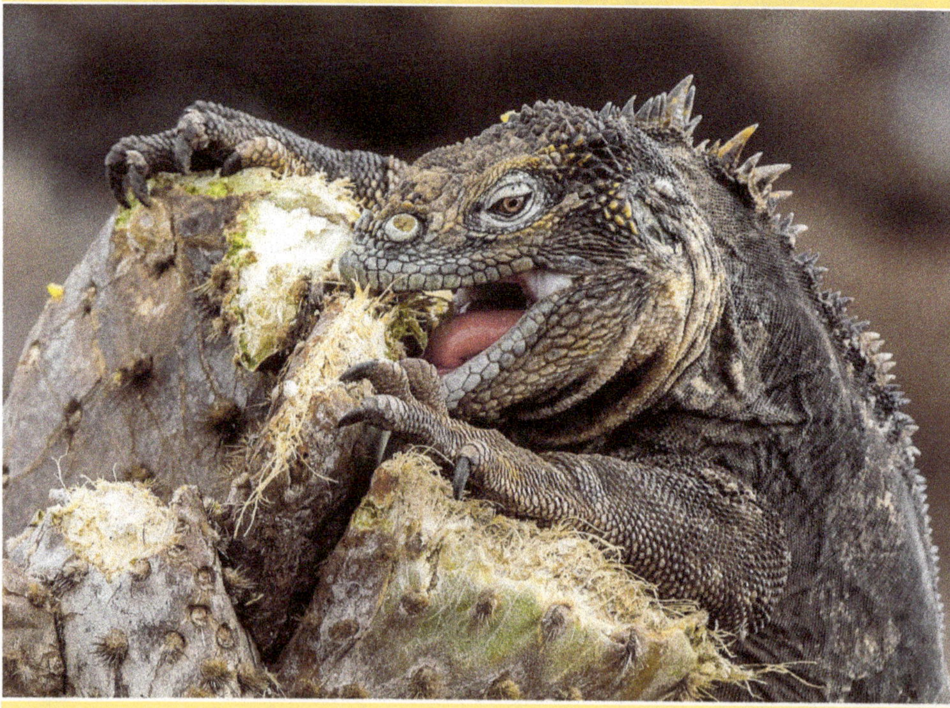

Galápagos Land Iguana

I could learn a lot from this iguana,
but, of course, I won't.
I can't sit still that long.
I want what I want when I wanna.
On a whim.

And there's nothing there
to tempt me, surrounded by the sea
like a castaway among some bugs
and lava rocks and prayer.
It's rather grim.

Weeks into a drought
he's still waiting under a cactus
for one of its pads to drop,
trusting everything will work out.
Good for him.

About 80% of the Galápagos Land Iguana's diet comes from the prickly pear cactus. Everything is consumed: flowers, fruit, pads, even spines. And it's his major source of moisture.

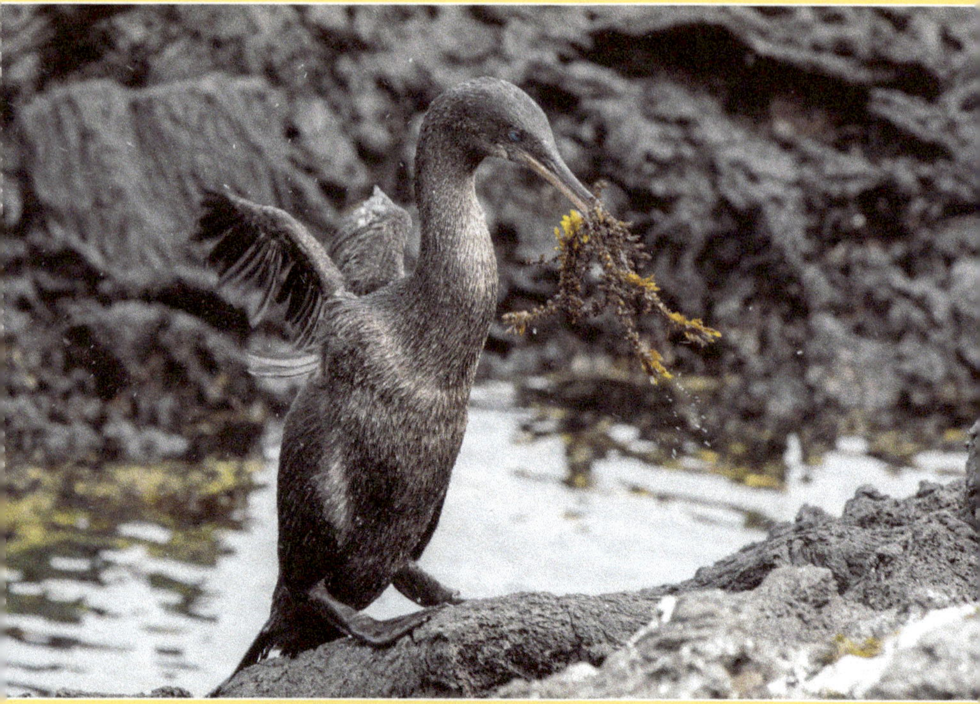
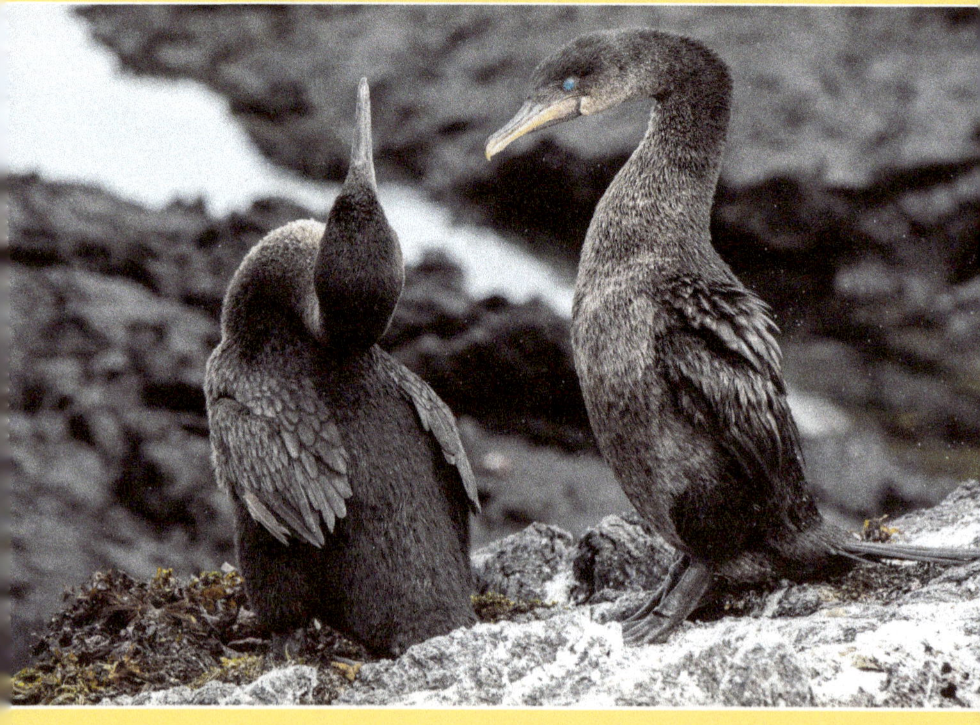

Flightless Cormorant

Most days they stand beside each other
looking out at the sea, their stubby wings
constant reminders that their usefulness
was forfeited forever in eons past,
but they don't remember what that was;
just some kind of emptiness, you'd think,
hangs on their backs, itching to be filled.

They're looking to the future, that's what it is.
He trudges up the rocks with some seaweed
which his mate gratefully acknowledges,
adding it to their nest. Their necks snake
back and forth cementing their commitment.

Now they fly when they fold those remnants in
and dart like homing arrows underwater.

One of the world's rarest birds, Flightless Cormorants are found only on the islands of Isabela and Fernandina in the Galápagos. Currently, there are about 1,000 breeding pairs.

Darwin's Finches

Consider my sisters like finches.
Even Darwin would be proud
how they adapted to situations
given what their times allowed.

The oldest adventured in academe
and through terrain. The middle one
was once Homecoming Queen;
the youngest found voice in volunteering.

By now they've published books,
rescued so many stray cats,
even knitted the homeless hats.
(What if, instead, they'd been brothers?)

They found their own way to survive
their faults and use their gifts to thrive.
All became successful mothers.

Darwin's finches are a group of about thirteen species known for the diversity of their beak form and function, which have adapted to available food sources in the Galápagos. Belonging to the tanager family, they are not closely related to true finches.

Galápagos Sea Lion

If ever there was a joy gene,
it's found full expression here
in the shallows along the shore,
on the sands of the beach,
stretched out over the rocks—

twisting and turning, reveling
in the fluid motion, lolling
in the waves, bathing in the sun,
spinning and weaving playfully
as weightless water acrobats.

Everyone's born to show off
('Look at me. See what I can do.')
before inhibitions clamp down.
But here there are none to limit the fun
of being silly, acting young. 'Arf! Arf!'

If ever there was a welcome calling.

Found in all of the islands of the archipelago, the Galápagos Sea Lion is the smallest sea lion species.

Galápagos Penguin

The trick to sticking together
through thick and thin,
for all you skeptics out there
hesitant to hear this from a penguin,
is to share doing what needs to be done,
whether by hook or crook or fin.

We weather each day.
We don't stray far from home.
We come home at night and stay
put. We strive to keep cool
and not overheat,
so relish the rock-splattered spray.

It's vital to keep in touch,
but we don't say much
in words and such.
What could be said
that a look can't instead?
And we'd never divorce, of course.

Endemic to the Galápagos, this is the rarest penguin species. Galápagos Penguins mate for life. Currently, there are only about 1,000 breeding pairs.

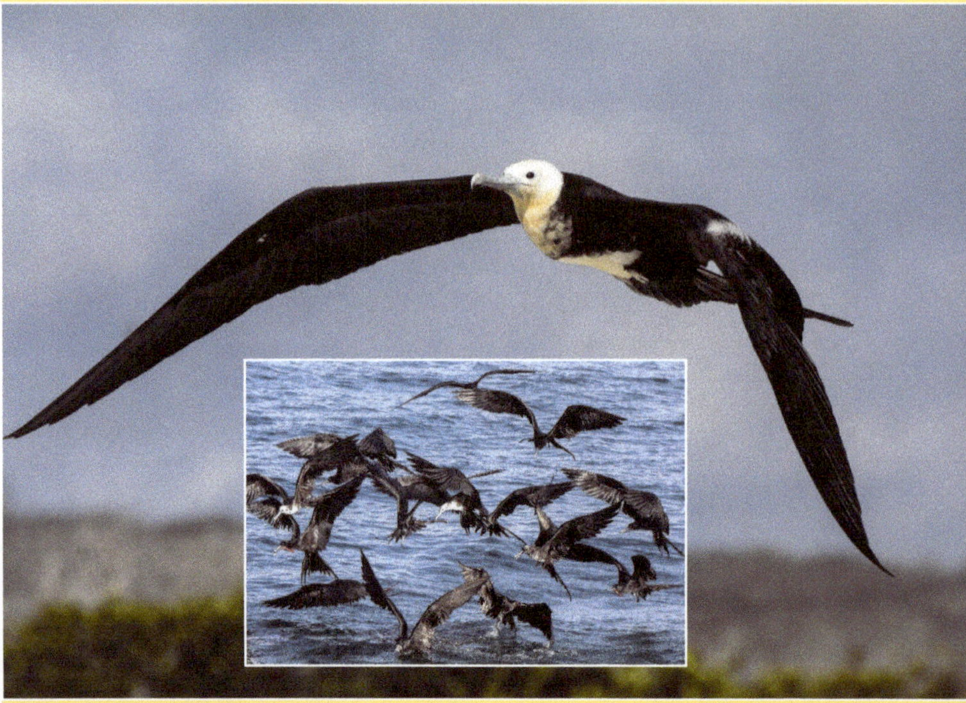

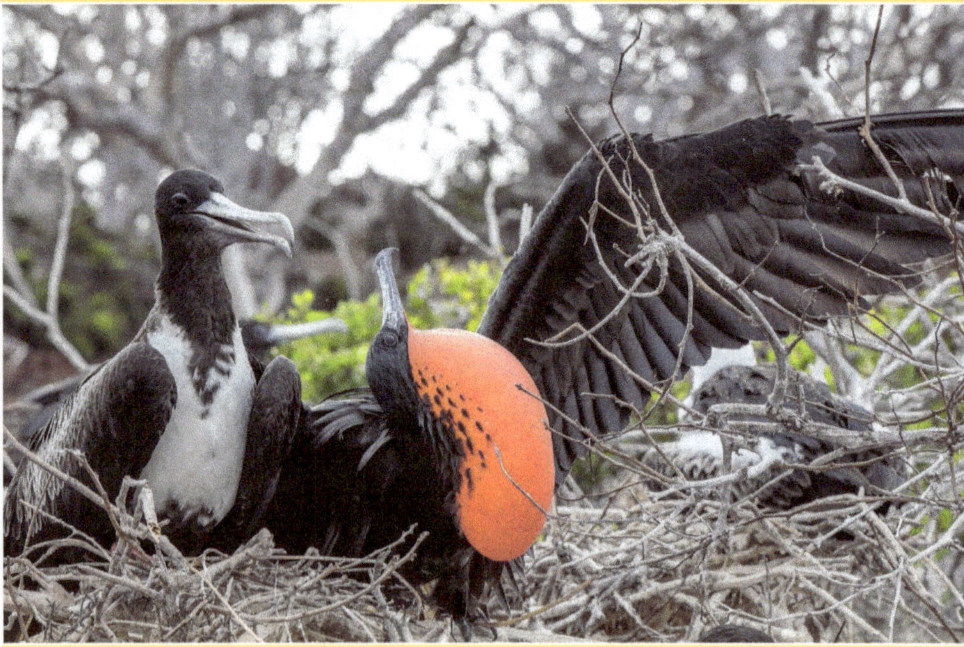

Frigate Bird

A pirate, a klepto.
A life on the lam
of grit and gusto.

A long, hooked bill,
snatching fish from the surface,
thronging to the thrill.

A Batman 'W' in flight.
Gotham in day,
grounded at night.

Seasonally monogamous,
raising a single chick,
then anonymous.

A romantic-minded male
puffing out his red pouch
to wow and woo. Ain't no slouch.

Frigates have the largest wing area to body weight ratio of any bird and can stay aloft for weeks. They are unable to land or rest on the ocean due to a lack of enough protective oil coating their wings.

Marine Iguana

Give me a rock to hug
and I'll be happy
to don my sleepy mug
and take a nappy.

Give me a band of blokes
like bros of a feather,
snorting salt, telling jokes,
chilling out together.

Give me beds of algae
between high and low tides
where I can shilly-shally
and eat my fill besides.

All I ask for is sunshine
and a lengthy shoreline
and a close-knit colony.
It's a hard life to be carefree—

but I'm warming up to it.

The Marine Iguana is found only in the Galápagos. Cold-blooded, it soaks up heat from the lava rocks and beach sand before foraging in the ocean, where algae make up almost all of its diet.

Waved Albatross

One of the last that will leave this season,
the big bird still sports tiny tufts of down,
plopped among the lava rocks like a stooge,
sleepy, pot-bellied, drawing the breeze in,
his wondrous wingspan yet to be unfurled.

He waits to be invited to the world,
unperturbed, harboring a lazy eye.
Who can judge now what will happen
when he wakes from this immature stupor
to find the vastness of sea, the soaring sky?

The Waved Albatross breeds primarily on Española Island in the Galápagos Archipelago.

Blue-Footed Booby

His goofy version of a two-step—
left foot up, pause, down, then the right,
head pointing to the sky as he whistles—
for the doting Mrs. by his side,
who, nodding her head, full-heartedly
approves the display, the magnificence
of the blue color redolent to her
of health and wealth and ooh-la-la.

Nature has a keen imagination.
From its color wheel, it chose between
the tender turquoise of the sky
and the aquamarine of the sea, just
where the birds will entertain their zeal
and prove imagination's real.
Still, some things are hard to imagine.
You have to see them for yourself.

About half of all Blue-Footed Booby breeding pairs nest in the Galápagos. The name booby *comes from the Spanish word* bobo *("stupid", "foolish", or "clown") because the birds, like other seabirds, are clumsy on land.*

Galápagos Hawk, apex predator

As many more individuals of each species are born than can possibly survive; and as, consequently, there is a frequently recurring struggle for existence, it follows that any being, if it vary however slightly in any manner profitable to itself, under the complex and sometimes varying conditions of life, will have a better chance of surviving, and thus be naturally selected.

—Charles Darwin, *On the Origin of Species* (1859)

John and Andrew, Darwin Lake, Isabela Island [photo by Omar Medina]

The Galápagos Islands, part of the Republic of Ecuador, are a volcanic archipelago that resides approximately six hundred miles off the mainland, straddling the Equator. In 1959, the Ecuadoran government established 97.5% of the land as a national park, only a very small part of which is open to tourists. In 1986, almost 30,000 square miles of surrounding ocean became a marine preserve. Movement of tourists in and around the islands is carefully managed and their numbers limited.

For fifteen days in December 2021, we cruised on a small boat among virtually all of the islands tourists are permitted to visit. Accompanied by a national park guide, we spent most of the time hiking and snorkeling and photographing wildlife—struck, no, touched by the efforts these animals had made to survive in the conditions they'd been given. Life adapts as best it can, Darwin noted long ago. Poems fostered by photographs seemed the best way to record our experiences. We hope you will have your own.

**

John lives in Port Townsend, Washington, and has authored several books of poetry, including *Waypoints* (2016), a collection of place-poems, *Twenty Questions* (2019), a chapbook, and *Delicate Arch* (2022), poems and photographs of national parks and monuments. Andrew makes his home base in San Francisco, California. His wildlife photographs were taken with a Canon EOS 5D Mark IV camera with a Canon EF 70-200mm f/2.8L IS III USM lens; underwater shots came from an Insta360 One X2 waterproof camera.

www.ingramcontent.com/pod-product-compliance
Lightning Source LLC
Chambersburg PA
CBHW040308170426
43194CB00022B/2941